UP A TREE

by
Kay Cheever

Copyright © 1995 by
KAY CHEEVER

ALL RIGHTS RESERVED

Library of Congress
Catalog Card No. 95-92597

ISBN 1-57579-005-X

Printed in United States of America

PINE HILL PRESS, INC.
Freeman, S. Dak. 57029

UP A TREE

Poems and Illustrations of
Relationship with
Trees, Cats and Auxiliary Companions
through Life.

by
Kay Cheever

Written and designed at
Two Arbors
925 5th St.
Brookings, SD 57006-2106
605-692-6533

THE AUTHOR/ ILLUSTRATOR

With professional parents and the youngest of four, Kay Cheever despaired of ever being as fast, as strong or as clever as those older. Words were the great equalizer. When eight-years-old she came home from school asking, "Should I just tell it or should I make it a story?"

As a very young child she would spend hours in her teeter-babe happily watching birch leaves shimmer. Adolescence found her climbing trees, increasing her perspective. Trees became a recurrent theme and emerged as a passion in bonsai, (bone sigh) the art of keeping trees in trays. Her articles have appeared in the American Bonsai Society Journal.

Trees are the largest living things on earth; plants, our only source of oxygen. Born and raised in Brookings, South Dakota she reminds us that on the flat prairie, trees not only lift our eyes, they lift our hearts as well.

Every cat she has ever met is unique. She was inspired to vent her sorrow through words upon the death of Fanny Flagg, an outdoor stray with an enormous tail. Other poems followed and the illustrations followed them.

Ms Cheever achieved a Master of Fine Arts degree and has received recognition for her weaving and dyeing. In addition to several solo shows, her work was chosen as an illustration in a book of contemporary work in fiber.

Ms Cheever was given a second chance at life when she received a transplanted kidney on July 11, 1983 at Mayo Clinic. She is most grateful to all who are willing to be organ donors.

These words were put together for personal pleasure. When encouraged to publish, she did. It is a way of sharing.

TREE TIME

Tolerant tree.
  Tree in a tree trance.
Yours is "timber time".
  You live in a time warp.

You cannot understand
  Minutes or hours.
You change only
  In decades.

Quickened only by
  The wind
Not fully asleep;
  Not truly awake.

Ceaseless change
  Unceasing.

STORIES

In our landlocked
Sea of grass, we are reminded of

Water by your trembling leaves
Which constantly whisper, sigh, shiver.

Do you tell tales of human longing
Or are these your stories you disclose?

What unfulfilled yearning does
A Cottonwood have?

Is it you or the wind we hear
Soughing in the boughs?

COMPARISONS

Arboreal rube.
Not much of a tree
Unless you have no trees

  'Cept Cottonwoods.

COMMUNITY

    Fluff on the wind.
      The cotton sticks to the wet
        Where they are wont to grow.
        Good for one; good for all.
          Community of Cottonwoods.

            Forestburg.

BREATH

Dispassionate tree.
   You are not inert.
Your frame mimics ours.

Trunk and limb,
   Foot and crown.
Vessels, skin, heart.

We breathe out; you breathe in.
   You breathe out; we breathe in.
We respire, you transpire.

Both rooted in *"spiritus."*
   Both rooted in earth.

When breath is gone,
   Life is gone.

WE CONSUME

Giants
We consume
Root, shoot, fruit, sap, seed.

We burn the very body in
Primordial rites of fire.

Arboreal bones hold the roof
Overhead.

Deep rooted, the ancestry tree can
Not run from our Greed.

More cruel than steel traps
Chain saws rip thru the years
Because we *Must Have More.*

Miracle of mouth to mouth;
Five billion breaths times
Ten times a minute.

The oracle of Dodona heard it
In the leaves.
We hear it
On the news.

Are we deaf?

DID A TREE JUST RUN BY?

You need no muzzle to still your bark.
You need no leash, you cannot pursue.

Neither can you flee.
You take what is given.

A one-sided bargain.
We molest. We consume.

We hew and you cry.
Arboricide!

What did the Druids know?

EACH FOLLOWS

Flower, fruit, foliage, frame.
Four reasons for four seasons.
Each follows
    each
        follows
            each.

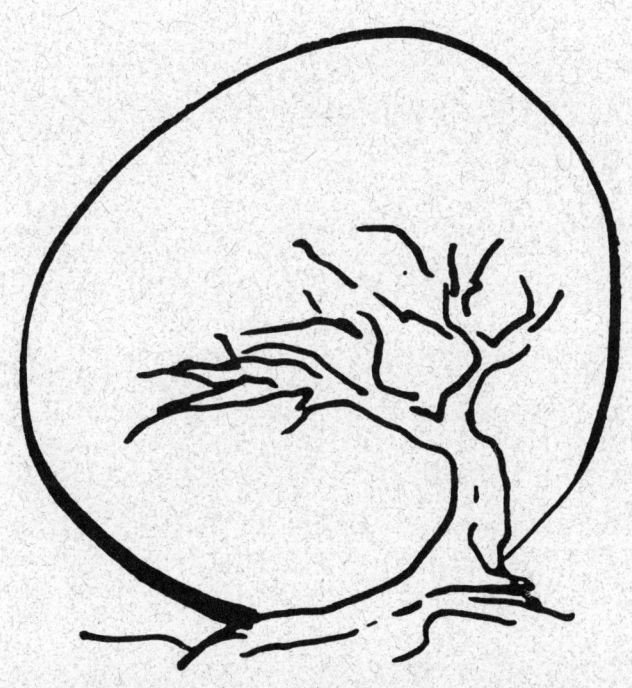

MAXIMS

"You don't have the sense
God gave to a tree!"

What would that be?

> *In a nutshell*
> *Branch out.*
> *Wave for attention.*
> *Bend in the wind.*
> *Stand your ground.*

There may be more sense here
Than we knew.

LITTLE TREE

Treelet with clay shoes
You move restlessly
around the yard
in and out of doors.

Do you yearn to be left
alone to set down roots?
Do you tire of constant
transportation?

FILLS US

The child who has a tough time,
The littlest kitten in the corner,
The puppy with the saddest eyes,

Melt our hearts.
The character who has stories to tell,
The old man overcoming adversity,
The lined face whose beauty shines forth

Draw us to them.
The tiny twisted captive tree,
Surviving on the margin,
Dependent upon our love

Fills our soul.

POWER PLAY

Dogs on leashes,
birds in cages,
fish in bowls,
plants in pots:

Captives for our pleasure.

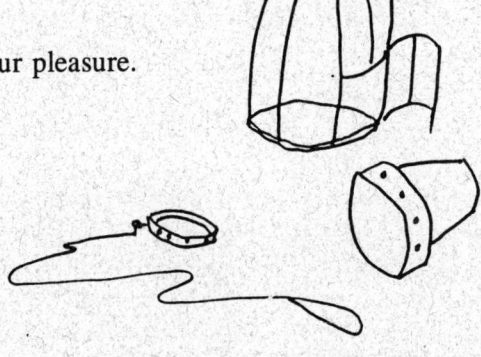

BONSAI

Bonsai is theater.
Bonsai is make believe.
Bonsai is playing with toy trees.

Bonsai is soul made visible.

FULL OF AWE

Trees are record of wind and storm
Sunshine and cold. They tell
Forgotten stories. So few live
To great age.

How awe full.

Wisdom does not make us old but age
Makes us wise if we are paying any
Attention at all.

How awe full.

Dwarf trees look old,
Seem wise, tell tales.
Bonsai trees are fairy tale trees.

How full of awe they fill us.

SOUNDING BOARD

Taciturn tree.
Silent sentinel.

Your glowing wood
Bound to
Clock chime, music box, harp string,

Reverberates.

Soul responds to soul.
Your voice is found only through

Sacrifice.

ICE TREES

Bright, brittle, glistening, crystalline
Glass trunk, limb, branch, twig.

Ramification amplified.
Exaggerated glittering detail in

Perfect attention.
Ice Trees.

Priceless.
Available at no cost yet

Unattainable at any cost.
Fortunately fleeting

Or we would have no breath.

BREATHLESS

Hoar frost.

White wisps
Of frozen fog
Fastened on every
Needle, tip, twig.

White on white on
White,
Blinded by beauty with beauty
With excruciating brilliance.

Gift of the morning,
Vanquished by noon.
Ravishing in its brevity.
Ravished by passage,

Immortal in memory.

SUFFUSION

Perfect whiteness.

Edge defined only by shadow.

Drifts drawing topographic maps.

Ice shadows, diffused light,

Efflorescent radiance.

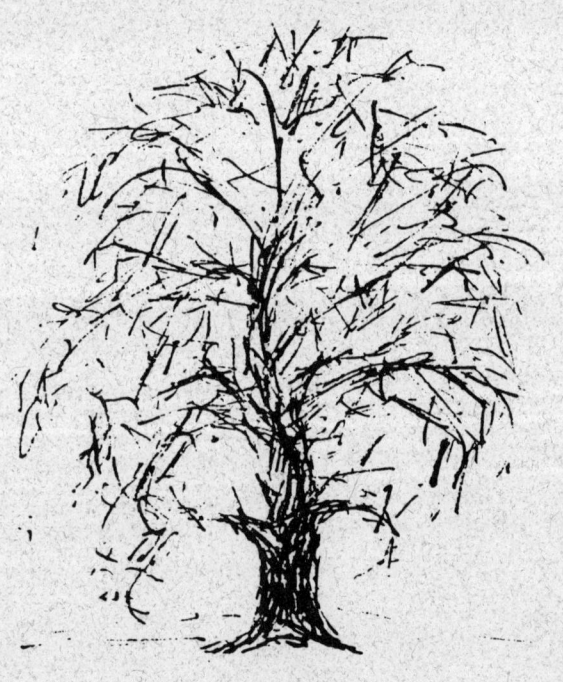

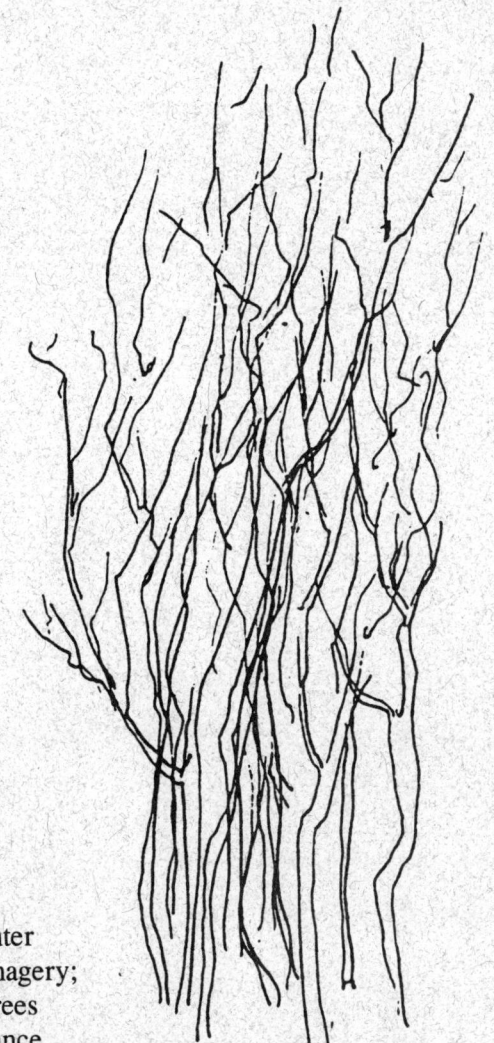

SPRING TO LIFE

Hope stiff with cold
Dreams of softer days,
Shorter nights,
Gossamer gowns.

    Struggle of winter
    Let loose by imagery;
    Supple green trees
    Rose red fragrance.

        Nests for hibernation,
        Torpid hallucination,
        Only memory remembers
        Anticipation of spring.

RELEASE

The whole great vast plain measured
In minuses for months. Stiff and latent
No body and no thing can flow.

"Slow as molasses in January." and
"As the days lengthen the cold strengthens"
Some old-timer said somewhere.

Until a magic March day
When snow crystals too cold to stick
Suddenly soften, shrink, sink, vaporize.

Exchanging a colorless palette for a drab one,
Brown and dirty with no promise.
The springing to come is unfathomable.

THE LAST HOORAH!

"You know," she said, "There is a world
of difference between saying to someone,

*'You look like a breath of spring!' or
'You look like the last gasp of winter.'*

These are the days it's hard to
Tell which is which."

APRIL'S PEIGNOIR

In nakedness she sleeps,
   Hypothermic innocent.
Quickened by the wind
   Lanquishing limbs lift and stretch.

Intoxicated by the wind
   She spins and weaves a gossamer gown
And slips into a veil of blossoms,
   A morning dress, April's *Peignoir*.

Her bony frame, hard and strong
   Against the light
Is hourly softened,
   Thickened in fecundity.

Arboreal bones are eclipsed as
   Foliage fleshes out form.
After sex, after birth, after
   The tedium of August, comes

Funereal pyre, incendiary fall,
   Divestment of vestments.
The fired skeletal hulk endures
   In coma, in nakedness.

CHILDREN IN TREES

Children climb trees
to be held in strong arms,
a rough embrace.

Children climb trees
to be taller and stronger
than their parents.

Children climb trees
to gain a new perspective,
to see things differently.

Children climb trees
for the same reason they ride horses:
to claim that power as their own.

SCENTS

Autumnal equinox,
Line of demarcation.
Trees are your penultimate
Banner; illustrators of season,

Stoic reminders of sense.
Metaphor of death
I see, I feel,
I smell your fall.

FALL DOWN

The only forces nature knows
Are growth and decay.
Spring up. Fall down.
Preparatory autumn screams
Wild excesses of
The final fling.

Blaze of death called beauty denies
Defense against unspoken dread from the
Inexorable hard march of winter.
Flamboyant foliage fated
To fall to earth

To spring,

Again.

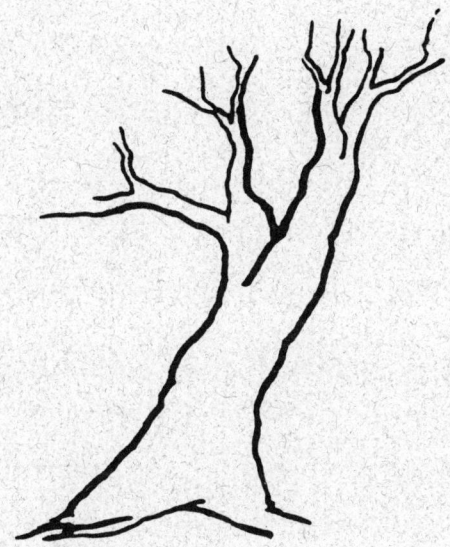

ABOREAL VOUYEURISM

I like winter trees against the sky,
I said.

What does that say about you,
she said,
that you like undressed trees.
A vouyeur.

They are pencil marks on gray paper,
each line in relation to all other lines,
I said.
They are structure, framework, rafters.
Arboreal bones.

I have never known anyone who
preferred bones to the flamboyant flounce
of trees in full dress,
she said.

Naked trees are the essence of trees,
I said.
The quintessence. They are the armature
the fabric of foliage is flung upon.

When spring comes, they stretch
their limbs, wakening, and slip
into a negligee, neglected, incomplete
attire of blossom and embryonic leaf.

Then, they dress properly for the season.
They seduce me no more.

Yes, I sighed, *I like to look at naked trees.*

WIPING

The cat came
Across the yard
And wiped herself
On my leg.

CATNIPPING

Patrick was an addict.
Mint was his downfall.
Got into the dried stuff.
Really had a ball.

He rolled, he frolicked
He buried his face.
He pounced, he scattered
All over the place.

He spooked at the air.
Heard nary a word.
He sank in a chair.
He slurred when he purred.

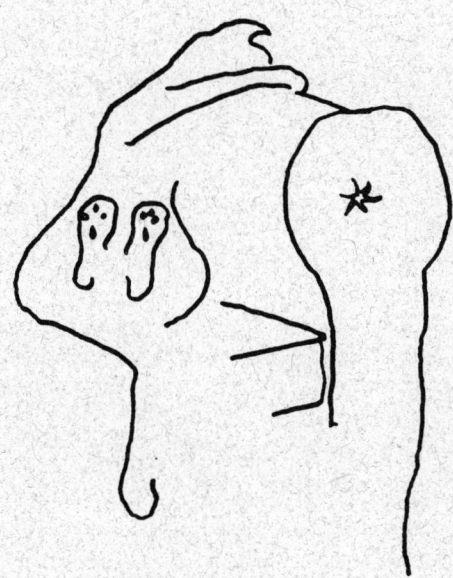

CATS AND CLOCKS

Clocks and Cats
  Cats and Clocks.

Their seconds are numbered
  Just like ours.

One second slower
  One second faster

And she would not have
  been there when the car was.

When the clock "dies"
  I take a key and wind it up.

There is no key for you my dear.

So many clocks.
  So many cats.

Who would miss one less.
    I do.

GIFT

She was just a stray,
   Detritus of the feline sort.

Cast aside intentionally or un-
    She drifted to our yard.

She chose us, she dropped anchor.
   Pretty Fanny, wet Fanny, lap Fanny.

She graced the garden for two summers
   Too sweet to last.

The intense presence
   Is now keen absence.

Her life, her choice
   A gift

Now gone.

IN AND OUT

They loved to hate each other.
Batted and hissed thru the screen door.
Even had to mend the holes.

The indoor cat in, the outdoor cat out.
Each happy where she was and
Happy the other was.

But outdoors is fraught
With danger.

The indoor cat keeps looking
But never

Forever

Will see

The outdoor cat

Again.

INQUIRE WITHIN

"Career Kitty" we called her.
She applied for a job we didn't know existed;

Rodent ridder, butterfly batter,
Viburnum napper, porch sitter.

How did we do it before her help?
Now the Garden is posted

"Help Wanted."
But who will come?

HOMINY?

The busy mother said,
"Yes, take a cat.
We have too many."

The child said,
in a soft but
measured voice,

"We have
A lot of cats
But not too many."

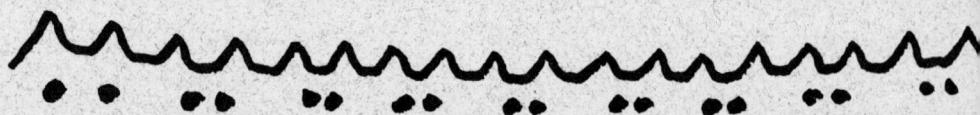

THE CAT WHO WENT TO CHURCH

    She scampered ahead
      Then fell behind and
        Scampered ahead again.

    Did she follow
      Or did she lead us
        To the church?

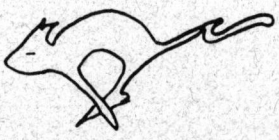

OMNIPRESENT

The faithful dog is called Fido
But it is Felix we should credit.

Watchful companion.
The ever present presence.

Chessy cat. You aren't ...
And then you are ...

There.

TRANSFORMER

Fierce, feral feline,
Never needing a hand

Is transformed
In an instant when

It discovers human warmth
And becomes

A push-over,
  A lap-cat,
    A pussy-cat.

CATS AND DOORS

Cats think of doors as
Options.

They want them all
Open.

Not to use but when
Shut

Both doors and options are
Useless.

RUBBER CAT

Rubber cat,
Not crystal, nor china
Nor calico.

You rub and rub
One side and
Then the other.

The ears
And back
Forever itch.

TATTLE TALES

I have a cat'O nine tails,
I have a cat with none.
I have a cat with one tail
And now my tale is done.

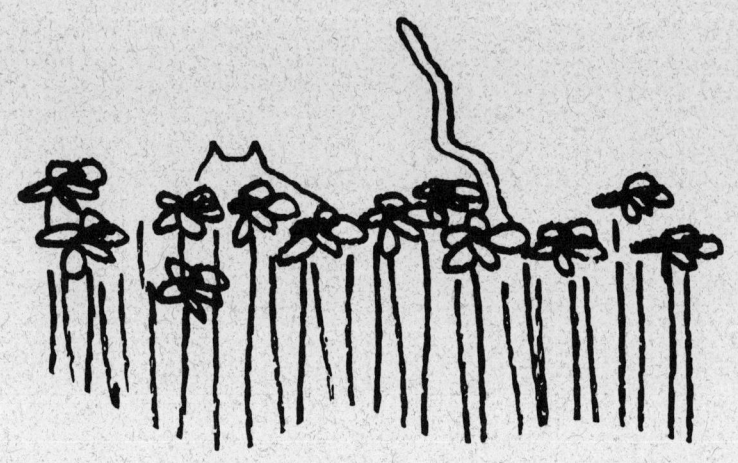

COME HOME

You've done this to me before.
I can't ride the roller coaster
So I got off.

You disappear for days
And then you reappear
Tail in the air.
What was my problem?

But you've been gone too long.
Oh Ivy, is it time to
Cry now?

GOODBYE IVY, GOODBYE

I refused to love her
For I knew she'd leave me.
But her crooked smile
Snookered me in.

And now the time to say
Goodbye has come.
And it is just as hard as
I had feared.

TOLD YOU SO!

I told you so.
I told you you'd get
Creamed by a car.
Why is there no joy in

Vindication?

PUBLIC MOURNING

How embarrassing.
To lose two cats in two years.
To have stood on the corner and
Rent my clothes and then
To do it all over again.

How embarrassing!

ROSWELL

The dead cat lay
By the side of the road.
The highway.

What low way
Did transect
So terminally?

And who is
Waiting,
Waiting?

SORROW

My friend's cat died suddenly last night.
What should I say? *That*....

  *.. he would be sad
     to see her so sad?
  ..there is another bundle
     of purr waiting for her love?
  ..he is at peace now, relieved
     of life's pains?
  ..he roams eternally in a field
     of catnip and voles?*

Such empty words in a now empty world.
Pain, so personal, so real,
   so hard to contradict.

Sorrow.

THE NEW CAT

Old treasures lost
Make room for new.

I named him "Mandu" for
I've always wanted a

Katmandu.

LIONESQUE

Gold'n white
Mimic of the tawny savannah
Pounces on movement
Invisible to me.

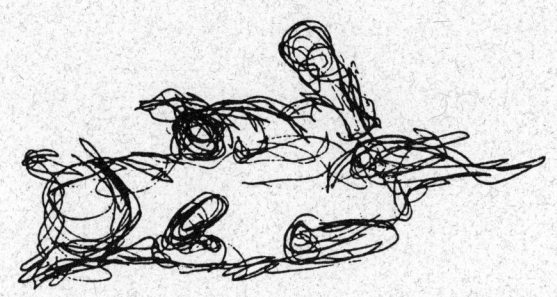

VERNAL EQUINOX

Tense from the cold,
Body held taut to prevent hurt,
Intense concentration to
Prevent that fatal slip.

As the valium sun grows
In strength; relaxing, releasing,
Exposing the vulnerable,
The grip loosens.

The outdoor cat flops
Against warm black earth
Unfolding,
Warming his tum.

RENALLY SPEAKING

Symbolic of the kidney itself
Many seeds mimic the form.
The "kidnal" shape of the butterfly
Proclaims the very resurrection.

Life from death.
The chrysalis.
The bean.
The cadaveric kidney.

Living death.
Life worse than death.
Life from death
Transferred and replanted.

The Seven/Eleven miracle;
Renal transplantation.

RELATIONSHIPS

How and with whom
we relate defines and
confirms our days, our works,
the loves of our lives.

Life is a gift.
My life is a joy.
The cycling seasons
and life
and death

confirm this.

FISH TALE

Large enough for a blind man to see
There in a warm, watery womb,
A kept creature for my pleasure,
Captive in a clear box.

Stupid mouth, silvery scales,
Tight skin over turgid body,
Silent, scintillating, circling form,
Flaunting a bridal veil tail.

Incredible, invisible, diaphanous
Tail, undulating, pulsating, propelling,
Purposeful in a meaningless place:
Ophthalmologist's aquarium.

RUMBLINGS

The summer storm
Muttered and muttered,

Unwilling to move on,
Wanting the last word.

BIRD CALLS

Dove of mourning
Your two note call
Calls to my soul.

Why am I moved?
Why does that lump come?
Is it that your

Haunting, hollow sound
Was the cup holding my
Childishly hurt feelings?

Are you unjustly linked to
Innocent summer play,
Tears and perceived abuse?

Poor bird. You are not depressed.
You've become the metaphor for sorrow
Through my own presumptions.

SPINNER

Teller of tales,
  How do you
    Spin a yarn?

The three fates
  Hold our mortal lives
    In their hands.

From unformed matrix
  Is drawn out
    Our story.

Whimsically, the
  Shears close
    Ending the yarn.

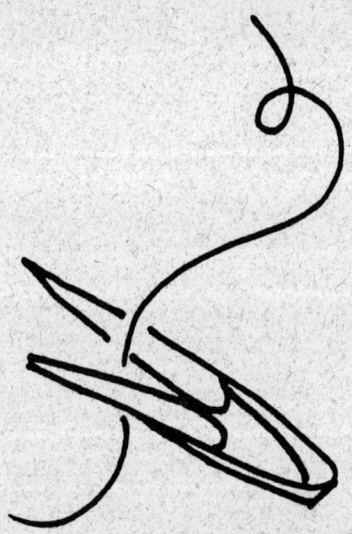

WARP AND WOOF

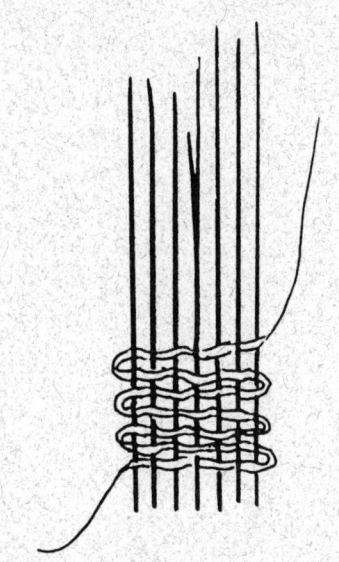

Weaver, what are
   Your elements?

The warp is the law,
   Immutable, ordained order.

The weft is life,
   Mercurial, spontaneous whimsy.

The fabric is our past,
   Flawed, textured, material.

The shed holds our future,
   Uncertain, unknown potential.

When will the Parcae snip the thread,
   Sever our mortal life, seal our fate?

Weaver of life
   What is your bias?

OBSERVED

Clothed in desolation,
shroud of grief.

Personal, palpable pain
left after love left.

Helpless, I can not
dilute the sorrow

to acceptable, imperceptible
parts per million.

I can cherish but not extricate.
That comes only thru grace.

THUD

What was that sound I heard?
The shattering of delusions,

A heart plummeting to earth,
The sound of inadequacy,

The discovery of error,
The given taken away.

Jumping to conclusions is
The only exercise I get.

That was the sound
Of reality.

WITHERING

Love is forever, eternal.
But *what* we love always leaves.

The item, the object, the topic
Is material, is fleeting, is grass.

Love entered the world when
Light was rent from the dark.

Love has always been for us to discover
But what we love always leaves.

HER/HIS/STORY

Historisity.
What a word to say
We all came from somewhere
Through someone.

We all have it,
Confessed or not.
Ignored
It bites.

Each of us boasts
A primordial mother
A primitive woman
Cooking with baskets
Fleshing with rock.

She could not live now
Anymore than we could live then.
We are shaped by our environment
But we bring to it our many mothers.

Our *historisity*.

VENERATE

My March skies abruptly lash
Smiles to frowns and
    Back.

Your August ones, so clear,
So steady, so
    Open.

My June, your December. Is it
The chemistry of age which
    Mellows

Or the reduction of
Energy or the wisdom of
    Experience

Which allows you to
Understand the moment's
    Trifle?

They say a woman becomes her
Mother. When will I achieve her
    Ken?

THE JOURNEY AND THE DESTINATION

You go on ahead don't
Wait for me.
I am spent.

I've gone as far and as
Fast as I can the best
That I can.

The wayworn way
We've braved
Has been salient.

I'll just sit here quietly
Amongst the fallen
Leaves and cats.

To lie fallow
In stillness
Is yet another joy.